NATURE TALES from OLD MILL CIRCLE

William Russo

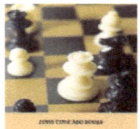

LONG TIME AGO BOOKS

A timeless tale of Nature unfolds among the small denizens of Mill Circle.

In this sanctuary far from the 21st century you will find the same activities that have bone on for centuries—long before people came as witnesses and destroyed the Yellow Spring. Here the chipmunks, squirrels, porcupine, hawks, turkeys, field mice, and geese, live out their instinctive lives, season upon season. Their conflicts and resolutions are documented in these short, poetic metaphors of a struggle small and unobtrusive, humorous and pathetic, ongoing on haunting Mill Circle.

Table of Contents

Yellow Spring

In the beginning there was but one mineral spring in Winchendon. It has been pluralized over two centuries, often thought of as Winchendon Springs, but it was always singular in its location. Fifty years ago, the yellow spring petered out, after being diverted and shut off by a local business decision.

The original medicinal water was the Yellow Spring, belonging to the Nipmuck native tribe of the region. And, when settlers came to found the town from the rocks and forest, they called the area Spring Village where, at first, some transient workers of a few sawmills chose to camp.

The ancient spring, known to the Pennecook and Nipmuck Indian tribes as the Yellow Spring for its coloration and unusual effects, quickly gained interest among the earliest settlers and explorers in the region then known as Ipswich Canada. Early reports stated there was one spring from which emanated water "impregnated" with iron.

The area was dangerous for settlers where it was described as an "unbroken wilderness" around 1730. Americans began to enter the territory around 1736 with an interest in building sawmills, using the abundant hydropower from the flowing rivers. According to one witness, the forest was dense and dreary.

Money was also offered to any person who would build a gristmill in the town of Ipswich Canada and manage it for ten years. Despite the uncertainties this was begun in 1758 and was a popular endeavor among early settlers and served as a major step to encouraging new families to move to the township and win incorporation into the Commonwealth of Massachusetts in 1764.

In the 1760s only a dozen families lived in the newly addressed township of Winchendon. Few of the houses had glass in the windows, but all were heavily fortified against attacks. The land along the New Hampshire border was an area where Indians fished and hunted. Trespassing was a risky business.

Traveling through this region was potentially deadly, and to venture near the famous healing spring of the local Indians could be considered a political provocation for attack. Choosing to stay overnight in Winchendon required "fortified" accommodations if you wanted to sleep soundly and safely.

One of the areas under Indian observation, the sacred Yellow Spring was a long-time gathering spot for Nipmuck tribes. By the end of the conflict in 1763, a veritable flood of British colonists came to the site of the flowing mineral spring. A few people with foresight thought it might be an enterprising spot for a spa and hotel.

Though the town area was not known for having abundant or valuable minerals, the spring's discovery by Native Americans and British colonists was the start of its reputation. One of the growing notions of the 18th century was the value of mineral water—and any location with natural springs became the resort of choice for well-to-do travelers. Iron-rich water was thought to have medicinal and health benefits that would restore energy to the blood and vigor to the muscle.

The yellow color to the spring came from its distilling through peat and bogs before it gushed at the spring. Modern witnesses who saw the last days of the old spring claimed that the coloration of water was not yellow, but more akin to orange.

The water gushed up hundreds of feet from deep below the ground, filtered through layers of rock and sediment. Though no harm can come from its yellow-orange color, such water may tend to stain clothing washed in it. The Yellow Spring provided all the locals their daily water needs—except for washing of clothing. The small bathhouse that was put next to the spring was for modest people to wash various parts of their body that needed a tonic to help restore their vigor and strength.

For many it was a long trip by horseback to fill a few jugs. First lodgings in the locality were to accommodate travelers who came a great distance for the waters and needed to rest over-night. Since many visitors were feeling unwell or had physical issues, the idea of a hotel near the spring was a profitable enterprise and began to be known as a hospital for invalids. Those who worked at the sawmill and later cotton mill were luckier, and their camps in the vicinity gave rise to a boarding house at Tolman's Tavern, said by some to have been constructed before 1800.

In the 18th century the notion of curing various ailments through aggressive use of mineral spring waters became the fashion. Physicians usually created a regimen of bathing and drinking spring waters every few hours. In Europe the great spas—like Karlsbad and Marienbad—led to the building of elaborate resort areas. In England in 1797 Dr. James Currie published a medical book recommending mineral water for its curative powers when used externally and internally.

Around the time Deacon White purchased the Healing Spring as part of his business, the city of Boston banned 'bathing' as an unhealthy practice. This attitude was short-lived as indoor plumbing became a more common feature of the 19th century. In Europe, the emphasis shifted to "drinking halls" where people were encouraged to drink mineral water. This may have been a rudimentary aspect of the spring hospital on Mill Circle and probably led to adding liquor to the water, hence transforming the hospital into a tavern.

With the popularity of spa treatment in the 1700s, many British colonists began searching for 'lost' or secret places with springs for soaking or sponge bathing. Hot water spas were preferred. Discovered locations for a spa by intrepid adventurers usually meant that treatment included a social life, creating an indolent lifestyle centered on the spring.

Twenty states featured such businesses that had a blueprint: a central two-story hospital unit near the spring with smaller houses nearby. Also recommended for full 'social' treatments for the community using mineral waters: buildings for dining, for sleeping, and for dancing.

Smaller houses were often built in a U-shaped pattern or semi-circle, and these little houses were guest cabins for wealthier patrons. This sounds like the blueprint for the earliest design of Mill Circle.

Perhaps out of the legendary belief in the healing power of gushing springs, more and more American adventurers learned of its existence from tribal natives and came looking for it. By the early part of the 19th century, the traffic to the secluded and difficult to reach spring had fallen off dramatically—but never entirely. Rather than medicinal or spiritual benefits, it was the hydropower of the flowing water that inspired businessmen to find the area to their liking.

Reached primarily by small, winding bridle paths through the 18th century, the land off the Millers River with its small pond shooting off Lake Monomonac mostly in Rindge, New Hampshire, and into Winchendon, led to an unobtrusive wayside inn. It was an oasis at the end of the wilds of New Hampshire as stagecoaches headed toward the metropolis of Boston.

In those early days before business came to the area and dug artesian wells to deflect the healing waters, the Yellow Spring became popular with its reputation for treating all manner of ailment. Visitors reported that the mineral spring spewed forth with thousands of gallons of water every day. Because of the frequency of the tribal use of the water, there were Native American footpaths coming from several directions to the spring.

Primitive means of crossing the brooks nearest the spring probably were the rudiments of stepping stone bridges that the 18th century sawmill would build and would be required to reach any inn or tavern. A small wooden footbridge forded the little stream at first. Elaborate stone dikes were later built to guide water flow around the sawmill area. Earliest businessmen realized that the waters might be reason for a hotel and tourism to occur at the town's fount.

In the decade before the French and Indian War, the Proprietors of the Winchendon area, called Ipswich Canada, made a concerted effort to bring more settlers into the area by seeing that a network of bridle paths traversed in every direction, making the land available for passage around the township.

Ten hardy, perhaps foolhardy families had taken an offer of £100 carve out log houses and open up the land, despite all the potential unrest with another war on the horizon.

Despite being free from war and able to be settled, the region suffered the curse of "remarkable events," as town father Ezra Hyde noted.

An early act of the new citizens of Ipswich Canada was to rename the Yellow Spring as the Virtuous Spring. The name change also could signify the victors' desire to put their own indelible stamp on territories once held by the allies of the British Empire.

The medicinal Virtuous Spring may have been a location frequented by people with frailties and illness looking for a cure to their medical problems, as well as adventurers seeking the fountain of youth. Reports noted that, for a time, the Spring was enormously popular—and an epidemic like dysentery always spurred people to save themselves with the iron-fortified waters of Indian lore.

Around 1772 ambitious and energetic Levi Nichols came to Winchendon and opened a tavern and inn, but not especially close to the Spring. The tavern and a foreign goods store were several miles from the Virtuous Spring, but reachable over rudimentary bridle paths, emerging from the footpaths of ancient native American visitors.

According to historian Ezra Hyde in his 1849 history, "There is a spring of the mineral kind, in the north-easterly part of the town. For many years after its discovery, it was called The Yellow Spring. It is of a medicinal nature, and rather seems of a chalybeate quality. It is not so much visited by invalids, as formerly." The Virtuous Spring was a cold spring with an iron flavor, less favored than hot springs by invalids and those with debilitating illness.

Considering the wilds and remoteness of Winchendon, Nichols took an aggressive stance and proceeded to construct what was a large and spacious facility. His foresight paid off because after the Revolutionary War, people began again to travel—and, according to observations by Ezra Hyde, "the tavern was well patronized."

Roads in the area still were primitive and poorly engineered. Of the pathway to the mill area, an early observer noted that the wagon would become stuck in mud, but "perchance of stealthy Indian on his tramp. It seems the very hatching place of theft. And murder."

Dysentery raged around the town in 1775 and could have been an impetus for patronage at the tavern and inn that Levi Nichols ran. It may have also contributed to the idea that a house was needed by the Virtuous Spring to shorten the trips by unwell people to the mineral water supply. With the demand for some cure or relief, patrons and locals might be drawn to the place serving the healthy waters from the Virtuous Spring. Having an establishment within walking distance of the Spring would be ideal.

Though the Virtuous Spring might seem to be a seasonal attraction only for summer and autumn, Nichols' tavern attracted a large winter crowd. At times there could be as many as "thirty or forty two-horse sleighs," around his house. His tavern was often filled with teamsters and the barn filled with horses. The spring's reputation drew drivers and produce wagons from as far as the Green Mountains. Hyde recalled the success of the place, "His tavern was for many years the most noted locality in Winchendon."

One of the first attempts to make a service of mail delivery and passenger service to the Winchendon area was started in 1795. Passing sleighs created excitement, as residents were thrilled to have mail once per week from Boston—and everyone rubbernecked at the visitors passing through the town. A four-horse stagecoach ran for a time, but patronage was not large enough for its continuation. The owner of the service complained that the roads were also in poor condition.

Coupled with the particularly bad winters that followed in the next few years, the yellow waters were more important than ever before. Whoever used the Virtuous Spring during this time also wanted it protected to extend its benefits to all those with afflictions. Historians like Hyde noted how immense snowfalls covered the ground and that the cold did not abate or melt for the entire winter. Hardship conditions increased around the renamed Yellow Spring in the early 1800s. Yet, it flourished.

Porcupine Alley

The Old Porcupine lumbers across the street at dawn.

Only in the fall are we awake enough at our coffee and breakfast to note his coming. There is no traffic at that hour on Saturday or Sunday morning, early.

We see him rarely because we seldom rise early enough to catch his meanderings. Can he instinctively know this? The old porcupine can be solitary most of the time. He likely has traveled this route for seven or eight years of the ten he may be allotted.

So, his plodding gait, shifting from one side to the other, gives the sense that he is carrying a too-heavy backpack.

No one and nothing requires him to rush. He usually also comes steadily into the backyard, along the stone path behind the house and comes out of the second driveway on the far side.

With coffee in hand, we can stroll to the picture window for our continued observation.

The porcupine has a silver back, which may denote he is of great age. We suspect he has come this way regularly for his entire life. He crosses the Mill Circle, but always assiduously avoids the plot of land where the haunted mansion once stood on his way to the stream down the slope.

Perhaps he thinks the haunted house is still there, or perhaps he is respecting its residents whose orbs float above the ground, in a corral, all night long, summer and fall, not just on Halloween.

The porcupine could cut across that empty plot and directly to the barn, but he never does. He follows along the outside of the corral, though its first slat is two feet above his head. It is the scenic route for sure.

He then reaches the old driveway to the long-gone mansion, and walks up that incline to the old barn that is the only reminder of a 19th century *grandeur* on the Mill Circle.

He pauses rarely as he wends his way to the far side of the barn and disappears down a slope. But, this fall, the silverback porcupine is not the one on the trail.

This season a dark black mass of porcupine quills follows in the same footsteps behind the house and across the second driveway and out to the circle. A younger and newer porcupine is not any faster in his dawn stroll than his progenitor.

He also avoids the corral around the ghostly field where nothing will dare to traipse.

No dogs, cats, deer, squirrels, chipmunks, or other mammals will walk across the place where the Old Manse once stood. It was thought to be haunted 200 years ago, and having been torn down makes no difference to the animals. They still see it looming before them.

Do they know the remnants of the haunted house were buried in its own cellar? Does something keep the porcupine from taking a short cut across that land? What do these animals know in their collective memories, or in their instinctual feelings?

Hawkeye & Squirrel Brunch

Just when you think the autumnal season will put a quick end to the animal wars of nature, you have a surprise over your morning coffee.

While sitting restfully and enjoying the view from the large window over the bistro table, we often take in the infuriating antics of the squirrels. Lately the plethora of leaves has made their made dashes a bit more chaotic. They seem to dig between the mounds of leaves that continually blow back over them. Two or three are now regulars each morning. We keep an eye to make sure they are not trying to climb under the car hood where they store propeller leaves.

This morning they were acutely active and unusually audacious.

Would the cold winds of December will be the only capstone to their nutty searches? How wrong could an observer be?

Looking away for a minute is a lifetime in the world of small rodents. My attention was caught by the fantail of a big bird. Ah, the turkeys had returned. One seemed to be rushing around my car, looking between the tires.

It was only when he froze in his posture that I saw it was a hawk.

And not far away, perfectly still, like a model for Michelangelo, was the squirrel. He did not even appear to be breathing.

The hawk twisted his head every which way before making another run at the gray squirrel who remained deep under my BMW. The hawk was not about to go under the car. He flew to a nearby tree branch where he could observe the squirrel's sudden movements.

Unbeknownst the the hawk, a second squirrel was on the opposite side the tree, clinging upside down for dear life. He would only move with the hawk was to move closer.

Of course, the hawk had his eye on the better breakfast squirrel under my car. The stalemate continued for ten or fifteen minutes—and the hawk disappeared around the other side of my house, but at a low angle. I thought he had not left the area—but was hiding.

He flew out again suddenly—and the squirrel was on the other side of a back tire, unable to see where the hawk was. This went on until the hawk flew off. For a long time, the squirrel was paralyzed.

On return, everything was still. Squirrels did not appear in the yard for the remainder of the day.

Turkey Trots & Crowing Rights

Well, the Clash of the Titans came early for Thanksgiving.

As we sat with morning coffee, looking out at our neighborhood Mill Circle, a holiday treat came in the form of a caged-free matchup worthy of the WWE. It was something to behold.

Not since the time we saw a couple of swans chase all the Canadian geese out of the pond have we been as amused. To see all the geese standing on the banks of the pond while swans glided around in glory was merely a preliminary bout.

Four crows took on six turkeys for grazing rights on the wild cranberries next to the old pond today.

The crows have been here since May, dropping by twice per day to cause trouble and have fun. We have seen them hopping up from the ground to tree limbs in rotation, like a competition or spring training. We have watched as they all stake out positions on the barn roof-- and reign supreme over our green Circle.

Earlier in the summer the crows and the Canadian geese would simply have a cold war. Each group eyeing the other, keeping far apart.

Yesterday for the first time six turkeys showed up, looking scrawny enough to escape this year's Thanksgiving dinner table.

These dumb birds don't really fly, but they leap up into trees in a single bound to sleep. They marched around without the organized grace of Canadian geese.

We believe the crows were simply looking for a fight, or hoped for an entertaining match to break up the day's boredom.

They would pop into the middle of a scrum of turkeys as they pecked. One leader would chase one crow till he jumped over him and to the other side.

Finally, two turkeys came after one crow, but they were confounded by the tag-team appearance of another crow. Two other crows watched from the trees, ready for their turns at the turkeys. Deflected to another bird, the turkeys in unison lowered their heads and charged like Teddy Roosevelt up San Juan Hill.

The crows took turns plopping into the field, causing the turkeys to create an offensive line with all six lining up—to come at the crows until the black birds leaped high into the trees, making their shrieking laughs at the ruffled turkeys below.

When they had their fill, the crows flew off with more mocking laughs. They had entertained themselves enough for this matchup. We anticipate more encounters.

Leaves & Leavings

Our New England neighbor from over the border in New Hampshire once said that "nothing gold can stay," and perhaps he meant the greenery of leaves.

We never see our grass turn to gold. It turns to brown, burnt by the sun. However, our leaves around the oaks and maples will transform for a few weeks into a lovely shimmering reddish gold before they fall to the ground.

At that point, they become tomorrow's task, and nothing but a greenback for the young men who come with their rakes and blowers to clean them up.

For a few days, these leaves, desiccated and dry, will pop around the yard, seemingly communal for they always gather in bunches in the corners of the house. They lay upon each other like brown flakes of snow, piling up as high as a window sill.

Temperamental, one leaf may jump around while others are still. It's enough to convince you that there is a chipmunk behind the cover. These dancing leaves tumble and rush like Nijinski playing the *Spectre de la Rose.*

Dead, they rise up from their damp graves on leaves of grass and fly in the face of anyone who wants to walk among them on a windy day. They may even tap on the window to catch your attention to say it's time to take us away.c

Bagged and bundled, they cannot stay here. They would overwhelm us every year until we were buried in their rot. So, they are carted off to some place where they can create lovely loam. When leaves are gone, you must live with their stark, empty tree limbs for six months until a new generation of buds make Robert Frost's green cycle begin anew.

Goose Lake

Where they nest is anyone's guess. It is likely on a small hill thick with underbrush.

We think the same couple of geese show up on the Circle every spring, with eyes for each other. If they mate for life, this would take up several decades. Now and then a third goose shows up, but is invariably chased away by the male. After a few days of this, the female joins in the chase to show her loyalty.

Only then do they seem to begin another year's family. Sometimes they have four or five goslings. This year has been a bonanza of child-rearing. The happy couple has their webbed feet full of responsibility with ten little goslings.

It is a mammoth effort of good parenting for a couple of geese to keep their brood in tact. Usually, somewhere along the line, we count the family and find one missing. Sometimes a second or third also disappears overnight. Is it disease? Predators? Or some other factor? We will never now.

This season they do not lose any of the young. Like drill sergeants they keep the big crowd in order. One goose is at the head, and another takes up the rear. There are always stragglers—and those are the ones who usually disappear.

The parents are dutiful sentinels. One eats while the other keeps out a hawk eye for those wanting a meal of young goose. They keep their gang in organized chaos. Naps come at mid-day for the exhausted children. They come close to the small pond, but never go in. They spend most of the time, picking and pecking around the tall grass. Only the tips of the grass appeals to their fussy appetite.

The grass grows tall as the goslings grow in a month to the same size as their parents. Still, the regimentation will continue until the leaves start to change, and the geese all start to flap their wings. Within a few weeks they will fly across the street, widening their territory.

An occasional run-in with the crows is never hostile. They stake out a territory and watch each other during the short meetings.

They stay together longer than most years. When they no longer make their morning march across the Circle to the pond, we think they have taken on independent airs. Yet, two weeks after disappearing, the group is back for several days, as if nothing has changed.

When the chill starts in the morning, we expect they will go away to their winter home. In spring, the same couple seems to come back. If any of their children decide to return for old times' sake, they are chased away. Another brood will take their place shortly.

Bird House Ghost Town

At one time, the plethora of various birdhouses must have been teeming with aviary lifestyles.

Perhaps there was a baby boom of starlings, blue jays, hummingbirds and robins, but that time has passed. Nowadays, the stylishly hewn bird houses are vacant. You couldn't let them if you banned cats from prowling the neighborhood.

What happened that the birds have chosen not to return here where berries, bugs, and flowers, hopelessly beckon. Was the address not as desirable as Capistrano?

Was there a murder in the neighborhood decades ago, as happened as the old Yellow Spring? After that, people avoided Mill Circle no matter how favorable the healing waters.

A catastrophe must have befallen the birds on the wing that there is no hospitality to be found among the few houses still remaining on the Circle. So, highly placed birdhouses remain empty, becoming shells of their former existence.

We have a ghost town of birdhouses on the street.

Bird feeding has fallen out of fashion. If you are not overrun by the clever squirrels finding new ways to break into the bird feeders and adjoining houses, you have the larger, more frightening notion that black bears will enter the neighborhood.

Warnings about feeding the bears, even inadvertently, has reached an audience that now stops putting seeds out for the migratory visitors. And, the denizens such as Canadian geese are not suitable for small houses. They need a large nest with three or four bedrooms for all their goslings.

And, so the birdhouse with the white picket fence nearby, and the house with the thatched roof, as well as the two-story replica of the Old Haunted Mansion, are ghostly reminders of a past when song birds would awaken the residents.

Now the houses are as haunted as the Yellow Spring. Soon, like the gazebo and Old House, they will fall into disrepair and be demolished.

If ghost birds haunt the circle, they are keeping the human ghosts company and maintaining the charm of the old haunt.

"The Haunted House, or The Mansion at the Spring"
Written by Zadoc Long, Jr., February 2nd, 1861

At a small opening, far away
In a dense surrounding wood,
Where wild beasts prowled in search of prey,
Lang syne, a dwelling stood.

A man of manner coarse and gruff
Kept entertainment there;
And on his door in letters rough,
Was written "Forest Fare."

'Twas when the country all was new,
Rarely a village seen—
Where early settlements were few
And many miles between.

A lonely spot, environed by
Rude nature's gloomiest scenes,
Deep pits and pools, and mountains high,
Steep crags and dark ravines.

Where had been found a mineral spring
Whose fame, sent far and nigh,
Did many curious strangers bring
Its healing charms to try.

The place became a choice retreat,
Where idlers loved to ramble,
And sporting characters to meet
To hunt or fish and gamble.

Carousels often held at night,
Loud merriment and jest,
Waked weary travelers with fright
Who put up there to rest.

When storms would howl and torrents pour,
And winds the forest stirred,
Wildly co-mingling with the roar
These revels might be heard.

And some, at length, surmised foul play;
Bloodstains had been discerned;
'Twas rumored strangers went that way
Who never thence returned.

That once retiring late to rest,
O'erheard, his bed-room near,
A cry of agony suppressed

That chilled his blood with fear.

The place so bad a name incurred,
It was at length deserted;
And not till long time afterward,
To any use converted.

The old house fitted up anew,
The wood-land turned to tillage,
The once waste now presents to view
A thriving factory village.

Its tragic mem'ries still beset
Some people living near it,
Who think the house is haunted yet
By that poor peddler's spirit.

And in the dead of night surmise
They hear unearthly groans,
The calls for vengeance that arise
From his unquiet bones.

Dire sights and sounds and strong accounts
Of spectres pale and grim
Are told; though wiser folks pronounce
These marvels all a whim.

Sure, he who now the mansion owns

(A noble-hearted fellow)
Keeps better things than dead men's bones
In his well-furnished cellar.

No skulking goblins harbor there,
No spirits but the best;
But it contains the choicest fare,
His friends can all attest.

About the Author

Dr. William Russo writes books on Hollywood history, biography, and nonfiction mystery. He held a professorship at a private college near Boston for several decades, and he has worked as a free-lance journalist for tabloid publications. He is a member of the Authors Guild, and he loves Mill Circle.

Books co-authored by William Russo and Jan Merlin:

     THE PAID COMPANION OF JOHN WILKES BOOTH
     TROUBLES IN A GOLDEN EYE
     MGM MAKES BOYS TOWN
     HANGING WITH BILLY BUDD
     THE ETERNAL CADET: FRANKIE THOMAS

Other Books by William Russo:

     AUDIE MURPHY IN VIETNAM
     RIDING JAMES KIRKWOOD'S PONY
     DUMB-FOUNDED: THE STORY OF AMERICAN LANGUAGE
     BOOTH AND OSWALD
     THE NEXT JAMES DEAN
     ALFRED HITCHCOCK FRESHLY SHOWERED
     DOCUMENTARY VERSUS DOCUDRAMA
     HAUNTING NEAR VIRTUOUS SPRING

For a full list of his entertainment writing, please go to *www.WilliamRusso.us*